GHOSTS

ANDREW CODDINGTON

Cavendish
Square

New York

CREATURES OF FANTASY
GHOSTS
BY
ANDREW CODDINGTON

CAVENDISH SQUARE PUBLISHING · NEW YORK

To Melissa. No Nightmares.

Published in 2016 by Cavendish Square Publishing, LLC
243 5th Avenue, Suite 136, New York, NY 10016

Website: cavendishsq.com

This publication represents the opinions and views of the author based on his or her personal experience, knowledge, and research. The information in this book serves as a general guide only. The author and publisher have used their best efforts in preparing this book and disclaim liability rising directly or indirectly from the use and application of this book.

CPSIA Compliance Information: Batch #CW16CSQ

All websites were available and accurate when this book was sent to press.

Library of Congress Cataloging-in-Publication Data

Coddington, Andrew, author.
Ghosts / Andrew Coddington.
pages cm. — (Creatures of fantasy)
Includes bibliographical references and index.
ISBN 978-1-5026-0932-8 (hardcover) ISBN 978-1-5026-0933-5 (ebook)
I. Ghosts—Juvenile literature. I. Title.
BF1461.C6377 2016
133.1—dc23
2015022188

Editorial Director: David McNamara
Editor: Kristen Susienka
Copy Editor: Nathan Heidelberger
Art Director: Jeffrey Talbot
Designer: Joseph Macri
Senior Production Manager: Jennifer Ryder-Talbot
Production Editor: Renni Johnson
Photo Research: J8 Media

The photographs in this book are used by permission and through the courtesy of: Jacobs Stock Photography/Photographer's Choice/Getty Images, cover; andreiuc88/Shutterstock.com, 2–3; © The Marsden Archive/Alamy, 6; Apic/Getty Images, 8; PM Images/Stone/Getty Images, 11; Thomas Northcut/Stone/Getty Images, 13; Photos.com/Photos.com/Thinkstock, 14; Photos.com/Photos.com/Thinkstock, 17; DeAgostini/Getty Images, 18; Utagawa Kunisada/File:Female Ghost.JPG/Wikimedia Commons, 21; freeparking :-| /flickr.com, 22; Everett Historical/Shutterstock.com, 28; Charles Temple Dix/File:The Flying Dutchman by Charles Temple Dix.jpg/Wikimedia Commons, 29; Frederick Simpson Coburn/File:What fearful shapes and shadows beset his path - The Legend of Sleepy Hollow (1899), frontispiece - BL.jpg/Wikimedia Commons, 30; John Greim/LightRocket via Getty Images, 32; John Quidor/File:The Headless Horseman Pursuing Ichabod Crane.jpg/Wikimedia Commons, 34; Lario Tus/Shutterstock.com, 37; © Mary Evans Picture Library/Alamy, 38; Mary Evans Picture Library/SPR, 41; Orhan Cam/Shutterstock.com, 43; By Ada Deane/File:Photo of Sir Arthur Conan Doyle with Spirit, by Ada Deane.jpg/Wikimedia Commons, 44; DEA/G. DAGLI ORTI/De Agostini/Getty Images, 47; Everett Collection/Shutterstock.com, 50; © Everett Collection Inc/Alamy, 51; © Pictorial Press Ltd/Alamy, 52; John Paul Filo/CBS via Getty Images, 56; mary981/Shutterstock.com, 59.

Printed in the United States of America

CONTENTS

The "Brown Lady" of Raynham Hall in Norfolk, England, is one of the world's most famous hauntings.

INTRODUCTION

Since the first humans walked the earth, myths and legends have engaged minds and inspired imaginations. Ancient civilizations used stories to explain **phenomena** in the world around them: the weather, tides, and natural disasters. As different cultures evolved, so too did their stories. From their traditions and observations emerged creatures with powerful abilities, mythical intrigue, and their own origins. Sometimes, different cultures encouraged various manifestations of the same creature. At other times, these creatures and cultures morphed into entirely new beings with greater powers than their predecessors.

Today, societies still celebrate the folklore of their ancestors—on-screen in presentations such as *The Hobbit*, *The Walking Dead*, and *X-Men*; and in stories such as *Harry Potter* and *Twilight*. Some even believe these creatures truly existed and continue to walk the earth as living creatures. Others resign these beings to myth.

In the Creatures of Fantasy series, we celebrate captivating stories of the past from all around the world. Each book focuses on creatures both familiar and unknown: the terrifying **ghost**, the bloodthirsty vampire, the classic Frankenstein, mischievous goblins, enchanting witches, and the callous zombie. Here their various incarnations throughout history are brought to life. All have their own origins, their own legends, and their own influences on the imagination today. Each story adds a new perspective to the human experience and encourages people to revisit tales of the past in order to understand their presence in the modern age.

A PRIMER ON GHOSTS

"Do I believe in ghosts? No, but I am afraid of them."

MARIE ANNE DE VICHY-CHAMROND, MARQUISE DU DEFFAND

GHOSTS, THE MYSTERIOUS FIGURES believed by many to reside at the edges of everyday life, have a long, rich history that stretches back to the beginning of mankind. The word "ghost" comes from the German word *geist*, meaning spirit or ghost, and the Middle English word *gaestan*, meaning terrifying. (Gaestan also gives us the word ghastly.) It is easy to see how these words come together to form the modern sense of ghosts as spooky, disembodied—or without a body—spirits.

Belief in their existence, however, is often dependent on a belief that after we die, the soul, or part of the body that gives life, leaves us and ascends into a world of the dead or a type of middle stage

Opposite: Ghosts roam the halls of haunted places well after they have died.

in the physical world—hence becoming a ghost. Without a soul, there can be no separate spirit to exist outside the physical body, and without a spirit leaving the body, there can be no ghost. Because of this, the debate over the existence of ghosts is usually closely tied to religious belief. Still, some people who were once skeptics and disbelievers have been known to change their perception after experiencing an otherworldly event. The question remains, though: Are ghosts fact or fiction?

What Does a Ghost Look Like?

Ghosts can manifest in a variety of ways. The most popular form of ghost is also the most rare: full-body **apparition**. As the name suggests, a spirit that manifests in a full-body apparition closely resembles the person's physical form when they were alive. The detail of full-body apparitions can vary. Some might appear translucent, or see-through, and vaguely humanlike in shape. Others might seem so lifelike that people who see them think they're looking at a living, breathing person.

More common than full-body apparitions are spirit **orbs** and mists. Unlike full-body apparitions, spirit orbs and mists are apparitions of spirits that do not resemble the person when they were alive. Instead, orbs appear as pale blue, semi-translucent balls of light floating through the air. Mists are similarly pale and semi-translucent, but appear like a cloud of fog. Because they are less detailed than a full-body apparition, spirit orbs and mists are often thought to be a ghost that has not gathered enough energy to appear in human form.

A spirit does not need to appear to a person in visual form to make its existence known, though. Ghosts might make themselves known through noises, such as knocks, footsteps, whistles, and voices; smells, such as sulfur or perfume that the person might have worn when they were alive; and touch, such as mysterious cold spots in an otherwise warm room, pushes, scratches, or breath on a person's skin. A ghost might even manifest by affecting a person's mood, causing them to feel more excited, angry, or uneasy.

Claims of the ghostly apparition of "spirit orbs" are common. They appear as pale, semi-translucent balls of light.

Ghostly Powers

Different types of ghosts seem capable of different powers. Ghosts are often said to be able to walk through walls and appear and disappear at will. Numerous stories of ghostly occurrences feature a witness who sees what might be a ghost and follows it through a hall or around a building, only to have the ghost disappear around a corner into nothing.

Ghosts also seem capable of other, more complex abilities. **Poltergeists**, which are discussed in detail in Chapter Three, have been reported to move physical objects, from small items such as books and silverware to larger items such as pieces of heavy furniture, levitating these items or sometimes throwing them clear across rooms. Some ghosts also seem to have psychic abilities, giving them access to intimate details of the people whom the ghost is haunting. Many cases of hauntings include stories of how the ghost knows a living person's name.

SEARCHING FOR PROOF

For about as long as people have told ghost stories, people have searched for proof of their existence in the real world. Part of the reason why the existence of ghosts is so difficult to establish once and for all is because of the nature of **paranormal** experiences. Ghosts frequently haunt secluded locations and typically appear at night when a witness's senses might be diminished due to the lack of light, grogginess, or fear. Additionally, ghost encounters are very personal, usually happening to someone when they are completely alone. This prevents the possibility of other witnesses who could confirm a person's account. Lastly, ghost encounters are almost always impossible to recreate, making it difficult to study them scientifically. Nevertheless, countless people throughout history have claimed to have seen or heard a ghost or experienced paranormal phenomena. The search for cold, hard proof continues.

Many people claim to have captured photographic evidence of ghosts, including snapshots of full-body apparitions, mists, and orbs. Sightings have become more common as photographic technology has become more affordable and more advanced. While there are a large number of alleged ghost photos, many of these have been proven to be fake, and the rest remain inconclusive.

Probably the most common category of ghost photograph concerns spirit orbs. These semi-translucent, pale blue circles appear in many photographs, seeming to float above people who are also in the frame, or darting across a corridor. While many ghost investigators are thrilled to have captured evidence of a spirit, it is very difficult to prove the authenticity of the orbs in these photos. Camera flashes reflecting off airborne particles or flying insects often create the same type of image, leading many skeptics to discredit the evidence.

Why Do Ghosts Wear Clothes?

Many of the most detailed descriptions of full-bodied apparitions have a certain thing in common: the ghosts are wearing clothing. One of the most famous ghosts is the spirit of Anne Boleyn, King Henry VIII's unfortunate second wife, who was beheaded in 1536. She is said to roam the halls of the Tower of London in her royal robes.

The clothing a ghost wears is often the telltale sign of the ghost's identity. Sometimes, as with the case of Anne Boleyn, the ghost's clothes allow witnesses to pinpoint its exact identity. Other times, people who stumble upon a particularly lifelike ghost might not know it was, in fact, a ghost until they realize the ghost was wearing clothes from a long-gone historical period. However, if a ghost is a manifestation of a deceased person's spirit, why is it still wearing clothes if clothes don't have souls?

That question has puzzled believers for years, yet no one has uncovered a reason. Some **parapsychologists** think they might have an answer, though. They say that a ghost might manifest in the same way that it imagines itself. If people are asked to picture themselves in their heads, for example, they typically imagine themselves wearing clothes—hence why ghosts appear to be clothed. Meanwhile, skeptics often use the clothing question as proof that ghosts do not exist but are instead created by a person's imagination.

Above: People who claim to see ghosts can often describe what the specters were wearing in detail.

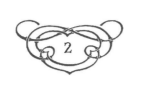

GHOSTS THROUGH HISTORY

"I am thy father's spirit,
Doom'd for a certain term to walk the night,
And for the day confined to fast in fires,
Till the foul crimes done in my days of nature
Are burnt and purged away ..."
THE GHOST OF HAMLET'S FATHER, *HAMLET*

GHOSTS HAVE BEEN A PART OF THE human experience since the very beginning. Over the millennia, the way humans have imagined ghosts has changed in many interesting ways. This process of reimagining and reinventing ghosts stretches back to the earliest historical accounts and continues today.

Ghosts of the Ancient World

While ghosts have existed in oral stories in many cultures for longer, the earliest representation of a ghost in literature is from the *Epic of Gilgamesh*, an ancient poem from Sumeria (present-day Iraq and Kuwait) that dates back over four thousand years. The first

Opposite: The ghost of Hamlet's father appears to Hamlet.

part of the epic poem follows the exploits of the mighty King Gilgamesh and his friend Enkidu. After Enkidu dies, Gilgamesh is deeply shaken by the fact that even a warrior as powerful as Enkidu must die. Fearing his own fate, Gilgamesh embarks on a long, unsuccessful quest to discover the secret to immortality.

In this final section, Gilgamesh thinks to summon the deceased spirit of his friend to learn about the fate of the dead. He asks the help of another hero, who makes a crack in the earth to release the "shade of Enkidu from the Netherworld as a phantom." The once-great warrior that Gilgamesh had loved so much appears beaten-down and distressed. "[M]y body like an old garment the lice devour ... is filled with dust," Enkidu tells Gilgamesh about his fate before falling to the ground with grief. When Enkidu recovers, they continue their conversation:

> "Did you see the one whose corpse was left lying on the plain?"
>
> "I saw him. His shade is not at rest in the Netherworld."
>
> "Did you see the one whose shade has no one to make funerary offerings?"
>
> "I saw him. He eats scrapings from the pot and crusts of bread thrown away in the street."

The impression in the *Epic of Gilgamesh* of the fate of the spirit of a dead person is a depressing one. The souls of the dead still seem to be present in the world, although in a different plane of existence than living, breathing mortals. These "shades," as they're called, do not seem to have any influence on the mortal world, but they are still tethered to the activities of their surviving relatives.

The Greek goddess Hecate (*standing at left*) was the goddess of the dead, witchcraft, and ghosts, among other things.

The spirits of those bodies who go unburied are subject to an afterlife of torture and misery.

The qualities of the ghost in the *Epic of Gilgamesh* are shared among other texts from other parts of the ancient Mediterranean, including the ancient Greek epics the *Iliad* and the *Odyssey* by Homer, and the ancient Roman *Aeneid* by Virgil. In both the *Odyssey* and the *Aeneid*, the living heroes visit the underworld to learn of the fates of companions who were lost at sea. Both accounts depict a shadowy world inhabited largely by tortured spirits. When the heroes find their lost companions, the ghosts beg to have their bodies recovered and properly buried to ease their spirits' suffering in the afterlife.

Early Modern Ghosts

The idea that ghosts were pitiable creatures that came out of the ancient Mediterranean remained the norm until the early modern period, which lasted roughly between 1400 and 1800 CE. During this period, writers such as William Shakespeare offered a new interpretation of ghosts. Unlike the powerless spirits found in the

Odyssey or the *Epic of Gilgamesh*, the ghosts of the early modern era are very active in the mortal world. Whereas the ancient ghosts were obsessed with how their bodies were treated after they died, these new ghosts seem concerned with one thing: revenge.

The vengeful ghost is a common character in the plays of William Shakespeare. In many of Shakespeare's works, the ghosts are the spirits of murdered characters, usually kings and other elites. In *Julius Caesar*, the ghost of Caesar appears to Brutus, the traitorous leader of the assassins who murdered him. Caesar's apparition comes the night before a battle between Brutus and Mark Antony, and Brutus takes Caesar's appearance as an omen of his coming doom.

The ghosts in *Hamlet* and *Macbeth*, on the other hand, do not stand idly by, filling the living with feelings of doom. Instead, they actually haunt the living until the crimes that led to their untimely deaths are avenged. In *Hamlet*, the ghost of Hamlet's father tells his son to murder Hamlet's uncle, who killed Hamlet's father in order to become king. In *Macbeth*, meanwhile, ghostly apparitions are numerous. The ghost of Banquo silently tortures his murderer, Macbeth, for his crime. Meanwhile, Lady Macbeth, who had urged her husband to murder Banquo and King Duncan, famously sees her hands and clothes covered in blood, invisible to everyone else but her.

The Enlightenment

Ghosts lost much of their relevance in Europe during the **Enlightenment**. Also called the age of reason, the Enlightenment began in the mid-seventeenth century. During this time, thinkers such as the British scientist Francis Bacon, the French philosopher Voltaire, and the German philosopher Immanuel Kant emphasized the importance of human reason. The writings that came out of that period spread across the world, including to the newly founded colonies in the Americas. They advocated that knowledge be based on **empiricism**, or observations that can be verified and repeated through experiment. Because accounts of hauntings could not stand up to the strictly scientific testing of the Enlightenment, believing in ghosts became laughable among Europe's educated elite—a stigma that continues today.

Nevertheless, despite this age of reason, stories about ghosts, witches, and demons continued to be told among the lower classes. In fact, some church ministers even encouraged their congregations to spread ghost stories to counteract the rise of atheism, or the belief that there is no god, which was becoming common as Enlightenment thinking spread.

Modern Science and Ghosts

Although science seemed to have replaced ghost belief following the Enlightenment, some people sought to use scientific research methods to study ghostly phenomena. These people are called parapsychologists. Rather than dismiss the existence of ghosts, parapsychologists try to apply scientific study through experiments as best they can to explain seemingly unexplainable happenings.

Recently, parapsychologists have used their understanding to propose a new theory as to the nature of ghosts. This theory holds that a ghost is a manifestation, or real form, of leftover energy, which explains why ghosts are often associated with particular places that have experienced tragedy, such as the scene of a murder. These events are highly charged with emotional energy left by people or things that experienced the event. Parapsychologists believe this energy can latch onto the surrounding environment. Sometimes this energy appears in strange ways—whispers, creaking, even shadows.

In 1882, several scientists and scholars interested in the paranormal founded the Society for Psychical Research in London. Since then, numerous similar societies have cropped up all over the world, and many are still in operation. Although parapsychology has gone a long way toward legitimizing ghost belief, it is still considered a pseudoscience, or fake science, because it does not strictly follow the accepted methods of scientific inquiry.

The Yurei: Ghosts of Japan

Japan has a particularly rich and terrifying tradition of ghosts, which in that country are called *yurei*, or "dim spirits." Like many Western traditions, the Japanese believe every human being has a soul, or *reikon*, which leaves the body when a person dies. From there, the reikon resides in **purgatory**, which is another realm of being between the physical world and heaven. When the reikon's relatives perform the appropriate funeral rites, the reikon moves on. If, however, the person has died violently, such as through murder, the family has been unable or unwilling to perform the funeral rites, or the spirit is motivated by especially strong emotions, the reikon may instead become a yurei and return to the physical world to haunt the living.

Because there are many reasons why a reikon might become a yurei, there are many different types of yurei. An *onryo*, for example, is a vengeful ghost, while an *ubume* is a mother ghost who died in childbirth and returns to care for her children, sometimes leaving gifts of candy. An especially unique type of yurei is the *funayurei*, which is the spirit of someone who has died at sea. A funayurei might appear covered in debris from the ocean, encrusted with barnacles or bedraggled in seaweed.

According to traditional representations, a yurei manifests in human form. A yurei is often described as wearing long, white gowns similar to burial kimonos. Its hair is long, black, and disheveled, and its hands are hung limply; its lower half seems to dissolve into nothing.

Above: Depictions of *yurei*, such as this one dating from the mid-nineteenth century, became a popular art form in Japan.

TYPES OF GHOSTS

"GHOST, n. The outward and visible sign of an inward fear."

AMBROSE BIERCE, *THE DEVIL'S DICTIONARY*

THE GHOSTS THAT HAVE BEEN DISCUSSED so far have been of a certain variety, usually called intelligent haunts. Simply put, these ghosts are the souls of the dead who have remained on earth, are aware of the living, and can interact with the environment and those around them. Intelligent ghosts are the most common variety of ghosts in literature, movies, and spooky stories. Chances are if you hear a story about ghosts or see a horror movie about ghosts, they are probably of the intelligent variety. There are many other types of ghosts, however, which will be discussed at length here.

Opposite: How They Met Themselves by Dante Gabriel Rossetti depicts a couple encountering their doppelgängers.

ELEMENTALS

As their name suggests, elementals are ancient ghosts tied to a particular natural environment, sometimes affecting and shaping the nature in which they dwell. These are often closely connected with paganism, either finding their origin in pagan mythologies or being the result of ancient pagan practices, such as human sacrifice. According to Robert Aickman, an English ghost story writer, staring at an apparition of an elemental spirit can cause immediate insanity in the viewer.

Elementals can take many different forms and have different powers, but a popular example of an elemental is the kelpie, or water horse, of Scotland. These spirits are tied to the waters of the many rivers and lochs in the highlands, appearing as beautiful black horses galloping along the bottom of the lake or standing on the shore. Some folktales say that the kelpie can also take human form, though keeping its horse hooves instead of feet. According to legend, the kelpie lures humans who wander too closely to the edges of the water with its beauty. Once the passerby pets or even mounts the kelpie, it dives straight into the water, dragging its rider into the deep. The kelpie's origins may have roots in Celtic myths about water gods. Then again, the kelpie may also have begun as a **cautionary tale** told to children to keep them from wandering too closely to deep or fast waters.

POLTERGEIST

The word "poltergeist" comes from the German word *poltern*, meaning to make sound, and *geist*, meaning ghost. Thus, a poltergeist is a noisy ghost. Traditional folklore holds that a poltergeist is a meddlesome spirit whose activities include creating loud noises,

such as knocking or clattering, as well as causing physical disturbances through its ability to, for example, levitate and throw objects. Unlike many other spirits, poltergeists focus on one individual rather than haunting a particular place. Usually, these individuals are teenagers, traditionally girls, whose emotional angst provides a focus for the poltergeist's energy.

Poltergeists are some of the favorite topics for Hollywood horror directors. Such movies as *The Exorcist, The Blair Witch Project, Insidious: Chapter 2,* and of course, the Poltergeist series draw inspiration from true-life accounts of poltergeist encounters. A poltergeist named Peeves also makes appearances in J. K. Rowling's Harry Potter series.

Doppelgänger

Another German word, **doppelgänger**, is translated as "double-goer." A doppelgänger assumes the appearance of a living person. The appearance of a doppelgänger has historically been interpreted as an omen of misfortune, especially death. A doppelgänger typically haunts the person whose form it mimics, but it may also appear to people close to the individual. This happened to the British poet John Donne, who saw his pregnant wife's doppelgänger before receiving news that she had given birth to a stillborn baby.

A famous instance of a doppelgänger encounter occurred to one of the most famous men in history, a president of the United States: Abraham Lincoln. In 1895, thirty years after the assassination of Lincoln, biographer Noah Brooks published the book *Washington in Lincoln's Time.* In it, Brooks describes a curious account that he claims he heard from Lincoln himself. Brooks documented the strange event, writing from Lincoln's perspective:

Ghosts are said to haunt the battlefields and buildings of Gettysburg, where over fifty-one thousand soldiers died during the Civil War.

the spirit is replaying an event which has already happened and in which the observer did not participate, it is not even aware of the observer's presence.

Such hauntings can range in size from an individual apparition to whole crowds of ghosts repeating events that have already happened. Some people who have visited the Civil War sites around Gettysburg, Pennsylvania, have reported seeing spectral figures congregating on the battlefields and around the historic buildings, sometimes several at a time, repeating the battles they fought and died in.

One of the most famous residual hauntings occurred in 1901, when two faculty members of Oxford University in England were touring the French palace Versailles. While walking through the stately rooms, they opened a door and discovered it full of people dressed in eighteenth-century clothes. They thought nothing of it as they walked through, thinking that they had accidentally stumbled on a reenactment. It was only later that they learned there was no such reenactment scheduled, nor was there anyone else in the hall they had been in. If the story is to be believed, all of the people the two professors had seen were in fact residual spirits, repeating an event that had long since passed.

Inanimate and Animal Ghosts

Some ghost stories do not feature the spirits of people at all. Many pet owners claim that the spirits of recently dead beloved pets have visited them. There are countless stories of people who have felt sensations of something rubbing against their legs or have even seen a full apparition of their deceased pet. Malevolent animal spirits are also a common tradition in many different cultures and are often feared for being omens of death.

Ghostly apparitions of inanimate objects, such as trains, cars, and ships, are also a common feature in folklore. Because inanimate objects, by definition, do not have souls or spirits, the existence of their ghosts is hard to rationalize. However, that doesn't stop people from telling stories of phantom ships and carriages. Perhaps the most famous legend about a ghostly apparition of an inanimate object is the *Flying Dutchman*. According to legend, the Dutch ship was sailing around the Cape of Good Hope at the southern tip of Africa when a great storm grew up around it, threatening to sink the ship. The details of what happened next vary, with some stories stating that the captain of the ship cursed God for the storm or challenged the storm, saying he would round the cape if it took him until doomsday—the end of the world. The ship never reached its destination, but is said to still sail the southern coasts of Africa. Anyone who sees it fears it as an omen of misfortune and doom.

Above: Sailors rounding the southern tip of Africa fear sighting the ghost of the *Flying Dutchman*.

THE ART OF THE GHOST STORY

"Another of his sources of fearful pleasure was to pass long winter evenings with the old Dutch wives, as they sat spinning by the fire, with a row of apples roasting and spluttering along the hearth, and listen to their marvelous tales of ghosts and goblins, and haunted fields, and haunted brooks, and haunted bridges, and haunted houses, and particularly of the headless horseman ..."

IRVING WASHINGTON, "THE LEGEND OF SLEEPY HOLLOW"

SOMETIMES, A ROARING FIRE AND ROASTING marshmallows on a crisp fall night just isn't complete without a good ghost story. For as long as people have seen ghosts, they have told stories about ghosts. These have grown into their own literary genre, or form, written by some of the greatest writers. Two of the most famous American ghost stories are Washington Irving's "The Legend of Sleepy Hollow" and Henry James's *The Turn of the Screw.*

THE LEGEND OF SLEEPY HOLLOW

The story is set just before the turn of the nineteenth century in Tarry Town (modern-day Tarrytown), New York. The quiet village

Opposite: The frontispiece to the 1899 edition of Irving Washington's "The Legend of Sleepy Hollow."

Ichabod kicked Gunpowder into a sprint to get away from the Horseman, driving headlong toward the church bridge where he had been told the Headless Horseman could not cross. Just as Ichabod was about to cross, the Horseman lifted the head from his saddle and hurled it at Ichabod. Ichabod tried to dodge the projectile, but it caught him squarely in the back of his head, throwing him from his horse and into the side of the road.

The Headless Horseman hurls a pumpkin at Ichabod Crane.

The next morning, Gunpowder was found grazing in front of Ichabod's hosts' home, but no one had heard from Ichabod. The townspeople searched along his route, following the tracks of two horses that had been pounded into the dirt. Alongside the bank of the brook, they found Ichabod's hat and the remains of a splattered pumpkin. Speculation into Ichabod's fate spread throughout the town. A while after the incident, an old farmer said he saw Ichabod in New York, where he had studied law and ultimately became a judge. Others suspected that Brom Bones, who went on to marry Katrina, had had something to do with the disappearance, but he never admitted to anything. In general, though, the superstitious town imagined that Ichabod's spirit had been carried away by the Horseman. It is thought that Ichabod's ghost haunted the old schoolhouse where he taught, which, without a teacher, had been abandoned and left to rot. On some still nights, one could hear Ichabod's voice singing a sad psalm.

The Turn of the Screw

The Turn of the Screw is told from the perspective of a young woman who has been hired by a wealthy London businessman to be the governess—a nanny who was also responsible for children's education—to his orphaned niece and nephew, Miles and Flora. The governess heads to Bly, the country estate where the children are currently living, with clear orders by her employer not to bother him with any news of the estate or the children at all. Besides the other house staff, the governess is isolated.

Once at Bly, the governess meets the children, who are both beautiful and charming. Shortly after arriving, though, the governess realizes not all is well at the peaceful country house. While outside, she looks to one of the towers of the house. Standing there is a dark figure of a man she does not recognize. When the governess asks the house staff about the appearance of the man, they say it must be the spirit of Peter Quint. They tell her that Quint and the former governess, named Miss Jessel, were favorites of the children. Both Quint and Miss Jessel were fired for participating in a forbidden love affair, however, and died shortly thereafter.

The ghosts of Quint and Miss Jessel appear around the house more frequently and more sinisterly, showing up on the opposite sides of windows and soon within the house itself. The governess starts to fear that the ghosts are trying to tempt the children to practice Satanism, or devil worship.

James's ghosts in *The Turn of the Screw* were of a different sort than those that appear in other works of the time. The ghouls featured in other popular ghost stories were usually either overly piteous, wailing of their misfortune for eternity, or exceptionally violent, seeking revenge against those who had wronged them in life. The ghosts of Miss Jessel and Peter Quint are neither of those. Their appearance is shocking, but neither seems to have a real physical effect on the events. The terror in *The Turn of the Screw* doesn't come from the ghosts but from the governess's imagination about and reactions to the ghosts.

Both Iving's "The Legend of Sleepy Hollow" and James's *The Turn of the Screw* have influenced later writers of ghost stories. Both take advantage of uncertainty in building the story's suspense. Ichabod Crane may have fled Sleepy Hollow or have been killed by Brom Bones, or he may have been kidnapped by the Headless Horseman. The governess may have seen the ghosts, but because no other person in the story can see them, it's possible that the governess is suffering from a mental illness. In both cases, there are perfectly reasonable explanations presented alongside paranormal ones. This spooky uncertainty has made its way into ghost stories ever since, and even into many horror movies.

Ghostly Urban Legends

Some ghost stories do not occur to an individual person or at a particular location, but rather happen all over the world to many people. These stories fall into the realm of **urban legend**. These stories circulate by word-of-mouth, are usually not written down, and do not have a clear origin. They seem to have come from nowhere. Many are said to have happened to someone related to the teller, and might begin with the phrase, "A friend of a friend …"

The many stories related to "white ladies" are examples of a ghostly urban legend. Nearly every culture has a legend about these ghosts. As their name suggests, white ladies are female apparitions dressed in a wispy white gown. Although white ladies are spotted nearly everywhere, from graveyards to huge mansions, many legends are set on remote highways late at night. A lonely driver traveling down a deserted road sees the figure of a woman standing at the side of the road. Some stories hold that the driver who stops to give this spectral hitchhiker a ride is never seen again. Others say that the driver passes the white lady, only to get a horrible feeling in the pit of his stomach. Looking into his rearview mirror, he sees sitting in his back seat the white lady, who suddenly vanishes into the night.

Above: "White ladies" are a common feature of many oral ghost stories.

SEEING GHOSTS THROUGH THE AGES

"During the day, I don't believe in ghosts.
At night, I'm a little more open-minded."

ANONYMOUS

GHOSTS DO NOT ONLY APPEAR WITHIN the covers of books. People have claimed to see ghosts in real life. These accounts span the globe and occur throughout time.

The Ghost of Athens

One of the oldest recorded "ghost investigations" dates back to the first century BCE and was recorded by Pliny the Younger, one of the ancient world's greatest scholars. (It was Pliny the Younger who gives us the most complete eyewitness account of the eruption of Mt. Vesuvius.) Pliny writes about a Greek philosopher named Athenodorus who purchased a house in Athens that was considered by many throughout the town to be haunted by the

Opposite: In this photo taken in 1891, the ghost of Lord Combermere appears to rest in the armchair at the lower left of the photograph.

ghost of an old man. Visitors to the home often fell mysteriously ill or sometimes even died, apparently because of the spirit that still haunted the home. Athenodorus, however, was not convinced. He bought the house and moved in.

Shortly after, Athenodorus himself began experiencing strange phenomena, including the sounds of moaning and rattling chains. Eventually, the ghost of the old man appeared to him in its full form. Athenodorus at first tried to ignore the specter, expecting the apparition to lose interest in haunting him if it could not scare him. However, Athenodorus noticed one evening that the spirit seemed to be trying to tell him something, motioning for him to follow. Athenodorus did, and the spirit led him out of the house, through the garden, and along an overgrown path to a clearing. Once the ghost reached the clearing, it vanished into the air.

The next morning, Athenodorus brought a couple town officials with him to the spot where the ghost had led him. They began digging and soon uncovered a skeleton wrapped in chains. The body seemed to have been the victim of torture and murder. The men exhumed, or removed, the body and gave it a proper burial. Afterwards, Pliny reports, the old man's spirit never appeared in the house again.

The Demon Drummer of Tedworth

One of the most famous poltergeist cases is based in the town of Tedworth (now Tidworth), England. In the mid-seventeenth century, John Mompesson, a local landowner and militia officer, intervened in the case of John Drury. In addition to committing forgery, Drury proved a nuisance to the townspeople of Tedworth with his busking, or his street performance, banging a drum throughout town. After handing him over for prosecution, Mompesson took possession of

Drury's drum, which Mompesson kept in his home. For months afterward, Mompesson and his family were beset by strange and alarming events. It seemed that every time he and his family had put out their lights for the night, the house would ring with knocks from inside and the sounds of drumming, which seemed to come from just above the roof of the house. Several times Mompesson tried to find the source of the banging, staking out the room where Drury's drum lay, but not once could he find the source.

This illustration of John Drury and his haunted drum appears in J. E. Smith's 1837 book *Legends and Miracles*.

Over time, the disturbances became more violent and invasive. Scratching sounds were heard around the house, floorboards were ripped up, furniture was thrown about the rooms, and in an especially distressing instance, a nail from one of the doors was driven into Mompesson's son's ankle when we woke up in the middle of the night to use the bathroom. All the while, the mysterious drumming continued. The noise at the house grew so boisterous that "it hath been heard at a considerable distance in the Fields, and awakened the Neighbours in the Village, none of which live very near the house," according to an eyewitness account.

Even today, it is unclear what caused the events associated with the Drummer of Tedworth, as the story came to be known. At the time, Mompesson charged Drury with witchcraft, but the court failed to convict. It is possible that the disturbances were caused by a group of Drury's friends, who conspired to threaten Mompesson and annoy his family. Another story held that Mompesson was summoned by the king, at which point he had admitted to inventing the haunting, using the **hoax** to encourage visitors to come to his estate.

Hauntings Around the World

Ghost stories are everywhere, from La Llorona, the "weeping woman" of Mexico, to Hanako-san, the ghost of a Japanese schoolgirl who was killed in a World War II bombing raid and is said to haunt the bathrooms of schoolhouses. Although people claim to have seen these spirits in real life, these spirits are often a complex mixture of eyewitness accounts, urban legends, and ancient folklore, creating entirely unique stories.

In the case of La Llorona, the general story goes that a woman drowned her children in order to be with a man. When the man refused to be with her, she drowned herself. Before entering heaven, the woman was asked where her children were. The woman realized what she had done and returned to look for her children. Now, she wanders the rivers and lakes of Mexico, wailing "*¡Ay, mis hijos!*" ("Oh, my children!") However, the story goes back further than that. In his book *Vision of the Conquered*, author Ángel María Garibay suggests that the roots of La Llorona stretch all the way to ancient Mexico and the gods and spirits of the Aztecs. One such god is La Cihuacoatl, or serpent-woman, who was believed to wander the streets of the Aztec capital Tenochtitlan, screaming, "My dearly beloved children, your departure is near!" Over the centuries, the ancient Aztec stories blended with other Mexican cultures, as well as with those of the invading Spanish, becoming the stories that we know today.

HAUNTED (WHITE) HOUSE

At the end of every president's term, he and his family must leave the White House in Washington, DC, to make room for the new first family. However, according to some stories, some people never leave the White House. These are the White House ghosts.

There are many supposed ghosts that haunt the White House. Dolley Madison, wife of the fourth president, James Madison, is said to haunt two locations in the White House, including the East Room, where she used to hang her laundry, and the Rose Garden. Mary Todd Lincoln said she could hear President Andrew Jackson stomping through the halls, swearing up a storm. First Lady Eleanor Roosevelt publicly stated once that she often felt a "presence" while alone in her private quarters.

The most active ghost in the White House, however, seems to be that of Abraham Lincoln. Lincoln's ghost has been sighted by many people including First Ladies Grace Coolidge and Lady Bird Johnson. Holland's Queen Wilhelmina has said that she answered a knock at her door to discover Lincoln's ghost standing before her. Prime Minister Winston Churchill of Britain also admitted to having a run-in with Lincoln. Once, after coming out from the bathroom, he opened the door to his quarters and saw Lincoln sitting in a chair by the fireplace. Psychics speculate that Lincoln's ghost is so active because he never got to finish his second term. Lincoln's spirit seems to be always on hand in times of crisis.

LIVING WITH THE DEAD

"It is wonderful that five thousand years have now elapsed since the creation of the world, and still it is undecided whether or not there has ever been an instance of the spirit of any person appearing after death. All argument is against it; but all belief is for it."

Samuel Johnson

F OR MUCH OF HUMAN HISTORY, GHOSTS in general have been viewed as unwanted entities that pester and sometimes even threaten the living. The Middle Ages in Europe saw the rise of complicated cleansing rituals that were developed to expel spirits and demons from homes.

Exorcising Ghosts

Perhaps the most common cleansing ritual is exorcism, which is performed in the Catholic Church. Exorcisms are primarily directed to expel demons that have possessed an individual person, though exorcisms have sometimes been performed to remove ghosts as well when simply blessing the house does not work.

Opposite: Sir Arthur Conan Doyle poses with a smiling specter. The famous creator of Sherlock Holmes was an advocate for psychic research.

In general, an exorcism happens when a priest directly commands the demon or spirit to leave the body or home. Protestants also had a procedure to drive out unwanted spirits, though it follows less of a procedure than Catholic exorcisms. Protestants typically sing hymns, sometimes for days on end, to force spirits to withdraw. (There have also been numerous cases in history where Protestants tried and failed to drive out spirits in this way and later requested help from Catholic priests to perform a formal exorcism.)

Western Europeans were not the only people to see ghosts as a nuisance or to develop means of expelling them. In Tibet, for example, people place "spirit traps" on the roofs of their houses. These contraptions, which resemble spindles wrapped in a web of brightly colored yarns, are thought to ensnare spirits who might haunt the family. When the trap catches a spirit, the family removes it and burns it, releasing the spirit and allowing it to be reborn. Similarly, many Native American tribes perform "smudging," the ritual burning of sacred plants. The smoke from the plants is thought to cleanse a person or location and drive out negative spirits.

Burials and Superstitions

People have been worried about the creation of ghosts for thousands of years. As seen in literature such as the *Epic of Gilgamesh* and in real-life ghost encounters, ghosts seem primarily concerned with the treatment of their bodies. When their bodies are not properly cared for, their spirits remain restless, unable to move on. Cultures in every corner of the world believe that the dead are to be respected, and these cultures have developed intricate burial rites to ensure that the deceased person's body and soul are properly cared for.

This Egyptian *Book of the Dead* detailed the steps necessary to ensure a deceased person's spirit transitioned peacefully to the "other side."

Many of these ancient practices continue today. For example, the burning of candles—a common feature in wakes and funerals—dates back to ancient times when it was believed the light produced by a burning candle was a talisman, or protective object, against demons. It was commonly thought that the period immediately after death was when a person's spirit was most vulnerable, needing to be protected at great cost. Candles came to be incorporated into burial rites to protect the body from becoming possessed and the soul from getting attacked by evil spirits.

The ancient Egyptians were particularly obsessed with the afterlife and ghosts, which led to the development of one of the most complex and detailed burial practices of any world culture. An entire book, called *The Book of the Dead*, was written to specifically detail and document every step that must be taken for a proper burial, as well as the journey the soul takes afterward. The Egyptians ritually **embalmed** their dead, crafted exceptionally beautiful sarcophagi, or coffins, out of rare jewels and precious metals, filled burial chambers with valuable artifacts and items thought to be useful to the soul in the afterlife, built huge tombs

across the desert, and protected these tombs with powerful curses to ward off robbers—all to ensure that the soul would pass on to the next world smoothly ... and not return to haunt the living.

Communicating with the Dead

The nineteenth and twentieth centuries saw an explosion of interest in ghosts and the paranormal in English-speaking countries, especially England and the United States. This rise accompanied the development of technology such as telephones and travel. As the world came to seem larger and more connected, people sought to find how they figured into the whole scheme of things. This quest for significance caused many to turn to the supernatural for explanations.

One of the products of this era was the rise of Spiritualism, the belief that the souls of the dead can and do communicate with the living. Later, **Spiritualists** also came to believe that spirits were capable of reaching higher levels of development and perfection than was possible in life, and that spirits could offer mortals advice on moral improvement.

The Spiritualism movement began in 1848 in Hydesville, a small hamlet in upstate New York. On that day, two sisters, Kate and Margaret Fox, made contact and held a conversation with a spirit, who responded to the Fox sisters' questions by way of knocks that were heard by witnesses. Spiritualism soon evolved into a full-fledged religious sect. Taking many cues from Christianity, Spiritualists congregated on Sundays to observe religious practices and sing hymns.

One of the byproducts of the rise of Spiritualism was the **séance**. In general, a séance involved people gathering around a psychic

Confusing Ghosts

Ancient people believed that sometimes even the best-planned burials could go wrong. Even when all the protocols were followed exactly, a ghost could still be summoned. The living took precautions to prevent being followed home by the dead. One tradition that may have arisen from this superstition is the wearing of black. The somber color has been associated with death in Western cultures for centuries, but it has been suggested that the reason mourners wear black is to confuse a ghost. A funeral attendant dressed in black was thought to be more difficult to see and thus harder for a spirit to follow home to haunt—sort of like ghostly camouflage.

Funerals in ancient Ireland took the idea of tricking ghosts one step further. People leaving a funeral often took a path home different than the one they had taken to the funeral. It was thought that doing so confused a ghost and prevented it from following a person home and haunting them.

People feared that the ghosts of violent criminals and witches could continue their evil acts even after death. Thus, the bodies of witches and criminals were often buried at crossroads outside of town in order to confuse the ghost, making it less likely that the specter would find its way back to town to haunt the living.

medium who would speak with spirits of the dead. There have been variations on the séance, however, using different tools, such as **Ouija boards** or musical instruments, to better commune with the spirits (or to entice new customers with novelty). Sometimes, the séance leader would even channel a spirit, allowing it to temporarily take over his or her body to speak directly through him or her. This was often accompanied by strange phenomena, such as distortions in the leader's voice or unusual body movements. Although versions of the séance had been practiced in many different cultures throughout history, the séance reached its highest popularity in the nineteenth century. People usually hosted séances in their homes, inviting the participants for an evening of entertainment and communion with the dead. Even Abraham Lincoln attended a séance held in the White House, which was conducted by his wife, Mary Todd, after the death of their son.

A typical séance involved participants sitting in a circle with their hands joined while a medium, shown here at the far head of the table, communicated with the spirits.

Another effect of the Spiritualist movement was the rise of "spirit photography." Using new photographic technologies, photographers would invite clients to their studios for a sitting. After the film was developed, a ghostly apparition that was not originally there would seem to hover near the sitter. Later viewers judged many such photographs to have been faked. One of the telling details was that many of the faces of the "ghosts" were identical across different photos taken at different times with different subjects, showing that the photographers were using tricks to create the pictures.

Escape artist Harry Houdini was a sharp critic of Spiritualism.

Spiritualism was not without its critics and proponents. Many respected scientists who investigated Spiritualist claims became converts themselves, including most famously Sir Arthur Conan Doyle, the physician who also wrote the wildly popular series about detective Sherlock Holmes.

Ironically, Spiritualism's staunchest opponent was a magician. As séances and mediums became more common, the talented escape artist Harry Houdini turned his showmanship toward debunking some of the most common tricks these "psychics" employed. Before he died, Houdini also made arrangements to conclusively disprove the existence of spirits after death. He left extremely specific instructions to his closest family on how he might contact them as a spirit. Some time after his unexpected death, Houdini's family confirmed that they had never once been visited by the ghost of their deceased relative.

SPECTERS OF THE
MODERN WORLD

"If there's something strange in your neighborhood,

Who you gonna call?

GHOSTBUSTERS!"

RAY PARKER JR., *GHOSTBUSTERS*

THERE ARE FEW LEGENDARY CREATURES as ancient as ghosts, and few have had the same staying power as ghosts have had. Ghosts still play an important role in everyday life. For example, in 2013, a poll conducted by YouGov and sponsored by the *Huffington Post* revealed that 45 percent of Americans believe in the existence of ghosts. The paranormal continues to be a source of inspiration for storytellers and psychics. The ghost story has evolved into a huge entertainment industry that makes its way onto both the big and small screens.

Opposite: The Ghostbusters (*from left*: Harold Ramis, Bill Murray, and Dan Aykroyd) ain't afraid of no ghost.

HOLLYWOOD HORROR

Since ghost stories are one of the most popular genres of fiction, it makes sense that they are also popular subjects for movies. Every year, dozens of movies about ghosts, evil spirits, demons, and possessions make their way to theatres across the world. The horror genre is one of the most lucrative for Hollywood studios. Horror movies tend to have one of the highest returns on investment, able to be made very cheaply while drawing huge audiences and raking in money at the box office. For example, *Paranormal Activity* (2007), a movie about a family documenting their experiences with a ghost that haunts their home and causes poltergeist-like activity, was independently produced for only $15,000. The movie made close to $200 million worldwide, nearly 540,000 percent of what it cost to produce, the highest return on investment for a movie of any genre! It's easy to see why: people love being scared. Many well-known actors also appeared in horror movies before they reached widespread fame. For example, Johnny Depp, star of such films as *Sweeney Todd* and the Pirates of the Caribbean series, found his first major role in the classic horror movie *A Nightmare on Elm Street* (1984).

One of the most popular movies about ghosts, surprisingly, isn't a horror movie as much as it is a comedy. Few horror movies—and few movies in general—have been able to compete with the appeal of *Ghostbusters*, released in 1984 and directed by Ivan Reitman. The movie stars Bill Murray, Dan Aykroyd, and Harold Ramis, who play three parapsychologists who start a ghost-catching business called the "Ghostbusters." Together, the three men, dressed like paranormal exterminators, do battle with an infestation of undead that is rampaging through New York City. Dan Aykroyd, who

cowrote the screenplay with Harold Ramis, had been interested in the paranormal since childhood. Aykroyd's father, Peter H. Aykroyd, wrote the book *A History of Ghosts: The True Story of Séances, Mediums, Ghosts, and Ghostbusters* about the journals that his father (Dan's grandfather) had collected about his research into ghosts and Spiritualism since the turn of the twentieth century. The movie was an incredible success and continues to find appeal over thirty years after it hit movie theaters. It has been named on numerous "Best Movies" lists and has made nearly $300 million worldwide since it was released, ranking it among the highest-grossing movies of all time.

Ghosts on TV

From the cramped drawing room tables of the nineteenth and twentieth centuries, mediums and other "sensitives," or people who claim to be attuned to the spiritual world, have used television to reach tens of millions of people curious about "the other side." Two personalities have emerged as the king and queen of televised mediumship: John Edward, host of the shows *Crossing Over with John Edward* (1999–2004) and *John Edward Cross Country* (2006–present), and Theresa Caputo, the subject of *Long Island Medium* (2011–present).

TV psychics have been a source of controversy since they first debuted. Those who believe say that mediums give their participants hope and closure with their dearly departed. Meanwhile, skeptics dismiss them as shams, saying that they don't actually communicate with the dead. Their practice of posing nonspecific questions to a wide sample of audience members, called "fishing," will always gather a positive response. These critics argue that the one audience

member who responds positively will actually unconsciously feed the psychic personal information, lending the psychic the appearance of knowing private information communicated by a spirit. Some critics go so far as to condemn TV psychics for dishonestly making a profit at the expense of their audience's unresolved grief and need for closure.

Shows about mediums aren't the only paranormal programs that have made their way onto the small screen. Paranormal investigators documenting their experiences as they search for evidence of ghosts have been the subject of numerous documentaries and television

Theresa Caputo (*left*) is the subject of the successful reality TV show *Long Island Medium*.

series. Shows such as *Ghost Hunters* (2004–present), *Ghost Adventures* (2008–present), and *The Dead Files* (2011–present) often feature teams of investigators using highly specialized equipment in allegedly haunted locations to look for evidence of the paranormal.

Spectacular Spooks

While watching ghouls on TV and in movie theaters may be enough to get some people's hearts pumping, others turn to thrill rides and ghost experiences for even more excitement. Disney's Haunted Mansion, located in both Disneyland and Walt Disney World, takes riders through the halls of a house occupied by the spirits of "999 happy haunts"—but with "room for a thousand!" On the more extreme end, though, true thrill seekers can sign up to tour a "haunted house." Every Halloween, thousands of these haunted houses crop up in plazas and shopping malls, offering thrill seekers the scares of a lifetime. Many historical locations also offer ghost tours alongside their regular tours. These are great opportunities to learn about a place's history—and possibly see a ghost of your own!

Ghosts have captured our imagination for millennia. They are both a source of terror and curiosity. The questions that ghosts pose are numerous. What happens to us when we die? Where do we go from here? The proof for ghosts will remain like the ghosts themselves: shadowy, visiting occasionally, disappearing often.

Organizing Your Own Ghost Hunt

The growing interest in the paranormal has given rise to a number of people, both amateurs and professionals, going on "ghost hunts." In addition to possibly finding evidence of the supernatural, ghost hunts are also a great way to have fun, explore a new place, and learn about its history. Here are some things you will need before heading out on your own "spook hunt":

1) *Permission.* This might be the most important thing you will need. Many haunted locations are owned by organizations or private individuals. Exploring a person's property without their permission is called trespassing and can get you into serious trouble. Always contact the landowner and get permission to look around before you begin your investigation. Owners can be a great source of information, too, giving you a clue to the location's history and the people who have lived and died there.

2) *Flashlight and batteries.* It's best to explore at night when the world is quietest and ghosts are thought to be most active. While a ghost encounter will surely get your heart racing, the environment actually poses the greatest threat to your safety. Moving around at night can be extremely dangerous, so be sure to carry a flashlight.

3) *Digital camera.* A camera is one of the best ways to document your adventure. Cameras also have the additional benefit of allowing you to review after your trip, capturing something you might have missed in the moment.

Many historical locations offer spooky tours, especially around Halloween.

4) *Digital recorder.* One of the most common ghostly manifestations is called an **electromagnetic voice phenomenon (EVP)**. While these phenomena are nearly impossible to hear with the human ear, digital recorders have been found to pick on these "spirit whispers." Recorders work best during question-and-answer sessions but be sure to ask simple questions and leave a long pause after each question.

5) *Notebook and pen or pencil.* Use a notebook to record details from your hunt, including maps of the location and times and places of unexplained occurrences.

6) *Friends.* What's more fun than getting spooked? Having friends around to share the excitement! Plus, you should never go into a strange place alone, so be sure to bring some good friends along.

GLOSSARY

apparition The appearance of a ghost or a ghostly image of a person.

cautionary tale A story told to warn the listener of danger.

doppelgänger German for "double-goer," a ghost that closely resembles a living person but is not that person's own spirit; usually considered an omen of death or misfortune.

electromagnetic voice phenomenon (EVP) Sounds found on electronic recordings that are taken as spirit voices.

embalm A process in which a corpse is preserved from decay.

empiricism The theory that knowledge comes from sense experiences that can be validated through experiment.

Enlightenment A period beginning in the mid-seventeenth century and lasting through the late eighteenth century when European intellectuals emphasized reason over superstition when it comes to understanding the world; also called the age of reason.

ghost A disembodied spirit, usually of a deceased person, that appears to the living.

hoax A trick meant to deceive someone.

medium A person who speaks to the dead.

orb A type of ghostly apparition characterized by a ball of faintly glowing, semi-transparent, usually pale blue light.

Ouija board A board printed with letters, numbers, and simple words or phrases that are pointed to involuntarily in response to questions posed at a séance.

paranormal Describing events or phenomena that are outside the scope of science.

parapsychologists People who study ghosts, psychics, and other paranormal phenomena.

phenomenon An unexplained occurrence that is observed by people.

poltergeist From the German for "noisy ghost," a poltergeist is a type of ghost that causes physical disturbances, such as knocks, bangs, or moving objects.

purgatory A place between the mortal world and heaven where spirits are sometimes trapped.

séance A meeting at which people try to contact the dead, usually through a psychic medium.

Spiritualist A person who believes that the dead can be contacted. May be part of an organized Spiritualist religion.

urban legend A story about an unusual event or occurrence whose origin is unknown; usually passed through word of mouth.

yurei The Japanese word for ghost.

To Learn More About Ghosts

Books

Clarke, Roger. *Ghosts: A Natural History: 500 Years of Searching for Proof.* New York: St. Martin's Press, 2014.

Dahl, Roald. *Roald Dahl's Book of Ghost Stories.* New York: Farrar, Straus and Giroux, 1984.

Newton, Michael, ed. *The Penguin Book of Ghost Stories: From Elizabeth Gaskell to Ambrose Bierce.* New York: Penguin, 2010.

Website

Your Ghost Stories

www.yourghoststories.com

This website is an excellent resource for all things ghosts. Explore some of history's most famous hauntings as well as accounts posted by users, read articles on ghosts, look at images, and watch videos.

Video

Ghostbusters. Directed by Ivan Reitman. Columbia Pictures, 1984. DVD.

BIBLIOGRAPHY

Anonymous. Trans. N. K. Sanders. *The Epic of Gilgamesh*. New York: Penguin Classics, 1960.

Aykroyd, Peter H., with Angela Narth. *A History of Ghosts: The True Story of Séances, Mediums, Ghosts, and Ghostbusters*. New York: Rodale Books, 2009.

Clarke, Roger. *Ghosts: A Natural History: 500 Years of Searching for Proof*. New York: St. Martin's Press, 2014.

Davies, Owen. *The Haunted: A Social History of Ghosts*. New York: Palgrave Macmillan, 2009.

Finucane, Ronald C. *Ghosts: Appearances of the Dead and Cultural Transformation*. Buffalo, NY: Prometheus Books, 1996.

Newton, Michael. *The Penguin Book of Ghost Stories: From Elizabeth Gaskell to Ambrose Bierce*. New York: Penguin, 2010.

Nickell, Joe. *The Science of Ghosts: Searching for Spirits of the Dead*. Buffalo, NY: Prometheus Books, 2012.

Norman, Michael and Beth Scott. *Historic Haunted America.* New York: Tor Books, 1996.

Index

About the Author

Andrew Coddington is a graduate of the Canisius College writing program and formerly worked in educational publishing as an editor. He lives in Buffalo, New York, with his fiancée and dog. He has toured numerous allegedly haunted locations throughout Western New York. Although he has never seen a ghost, he loves a great ghost story.